P9-ECP-365

The
Seeing
Eye

Also by Victor B. Scheffer

THE YEAR OF THE WHALE

LITTLE CALF

THE YEAR OF THE SEAL

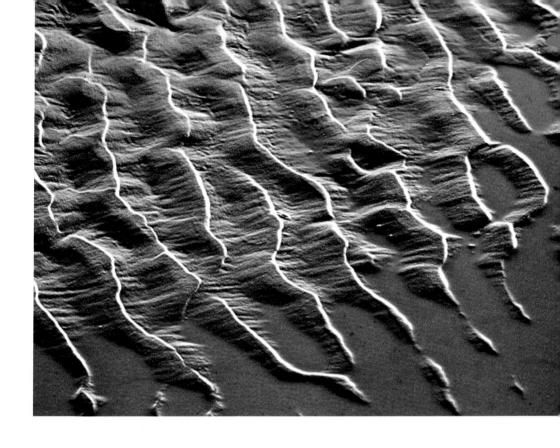

The
Seeing
Eye

words and photographs by

Victor B. Scheffer

CHARLES SCRIBNER'S SONS

NEW YORK

Copyright © 1971 Victor B. Scheffer

All the photographs, including the title-page photograph, were taken by the author
at various locations, including the Pribilof Islands of Alaska; the seacoasts of
California, Oregon, and Washington; the Horse Heaven Plateau, Lake Cushman,
North Bend, Wenatchee, Mount Rainier, Packwood, and Bellevue in interior
Washington. Nearly half were taken at Hilltop, a residential park with an
elevation of 900-1200 feet, near Bellevue.

Title-page photograph: Wave ripples on a sandy seacoast.

The diagram on page 21 is from R. E. Williams, "Space-Filling Polyhedron," *Science*,
vol. 161, page 276 (copyright 1968 by the American Association for the Advancement
of Science). Used by permission.

This book published simultaneously in the
United States of America and in Canada —
Copyright under the Berne Convention

All rights reserved. No part of this book
may be reproduced in any form without the
permission of Charles Scribner's Sons.

A—2.71 [PZ]

PRINTED IN THE UNITED STATES OF AMERICA
SBN 684–92311–4
Library of Congress Catalog Card Number 70-140773

This book is for young readers,
and for all adults who remember the bright,
sharp, wonderful world of the young.

Skeleton of an alder leaf (*Alnus rubra*) against the sunset

The Seeing Eye

When you learn to see what you look at in the outdoor world you begin to marvel at the forms and textures and colors of nature. You begin to notice that certain patterns are more interesting than others and to wonder why. And when you look time and again at fallen leaves all powdered with frost, and at porous gray stones at the edge of the sea, and at fruits of the wild rose burning roundly and redly in the shadows, and at a thousand other images of beauty, you are on the way to appreciation both of man's art and of his science.

For art and science have common roots. They depend on imagination, they use a searching approach to truth, and they use symbols—pictures and numbers—for explaining truth. Hidden within all of us are the seeds of creative art and science. Perhaps this book will help the seeds to germinate.

As you read, you will find that these pages call attention both to beauty and to deeper meaning. They suggest that, when you feel a quick pleasure at seeing some delightful image out-of-doors, you can also enjoy the reasons for its attraction. Though indeed the beauty of a seashell needs no explanation, you will enjoy it more if you know that its line describes a special kind of curve displayed in many other growing things.

Few patterns in nature are "random" in the mathematical sense. Most contain a kind of order which the well-trained eye can see. For example, you look at a beach covered with small flat rocks, and you think at first that the pattern is accidental. Soon you realize that the waves and the tides have sorted the rocks by size and have arranged them by space. If you tried to imitate the pattern, you would end with one that would have an artificial look about it. Or you study a grove of trees, thinking at first that they are spaced every-which-way. But when you look down on the trees from a hilltop, you see that they have regular positions according to the need of each for sunlight and moisture.

Today we are overwhelmed by examples of technological cleverness. On television we watch men shuffle in the dust of the moon. We learn that faint signals are reaching us from objects in the distant sky twelve billion light-years away. We learn that a rabbit can be taken from its mother before birth and raised in a germ-free chamber. We are impressed by the marvel of a tele-cable that can transmit a hundred conversations at once. We are deceived into thinking that man by himself can create a world full of beauty and comfort and happiness. Not so. All the experts together cannot build a single petal of a rose, nor can they build "something just as good." No artificial palace of pleasure can give you the special feeling you have when you lie all alone on the ground and smell the warm black earth and watch the tiny creatures of the grassy forest pursue their strange and separate ways. It is the infinite variety, and complexity, and mystery of nature that man tries to duplicate but never can.

You have probably heard the expression "nature's art." This is poetic; only humans can create and recognize works of art. The outdoor world is filled with patterns that are art sources but are not art. To be sure, you can easily find arrangements of

8

peeling bark on a dead tree, and bright leaves floating on a pool, and many other patterns out-of-doors that resemble paintings. In some modern paintings the artist tries to leave out all real objects, and in trying to remove or abstract nature, he produces what is called abstract art. Nonetheless, he often produces the kind of composition that a well-trained observer can see in nature.

The pictures in the book are grouped according to three elements of beauty: form, texture, and color. You will begin to understand these elements as you turn the pages. Though every natural pattern contains all three, one pattern may impress you most vividly for its form, another for its texture, and another for its color. The pictures are described generally in the text; the captions tell what actual objects in nature the pictures represent.

Shadows on a pebbly shore

10

Form

Form is the outline, the framework, the bone structure of the pattern in nature. A painter would say that form is the blocking-out of the lines of the composition, or the first, quick strokes of the brush. It is the plan.

On the beach at left an unseen tree is casting a bold shadow like a slash of dark paint on a canvas. The first impression is of shape or form.

In the picture below, the rocks are lighted by the early morning sun. Black shadows weave a fabric of forms. Turn the book around and look at the picture from any side; it is still attractive. It has balance, and balance is generally pleasing to the eye. There are bal-

Sedimentary rock in a creek bed

ances in nature between light and dark, between colors, between motion and rest, between violence and peace.

The form of the straight line has the special charm of simplicity. Did you ever notice the vertical line of the sun's reflection along the smooth body of a tree (right), or stop to enjoy the shine of a drift-log cleansed by the ocean waves (below)?

Turn the book upside down and imagine that you are seeing the tree reflected in a forest pool.

A log cast up by waves on a seacoast

Sunlight on the trunk of a wild cherry (*Prunus emarginata*)

Circles and spheres are common in nature. They often result from the radial growth of a plant or animal from a central seed or embryo. The gray plant shown below is a lichen (*lí-ken*) growing on the face of a volcanic cliff. Lichens are tough pioneers. They are among the first plants to move in when volcanic lava has cooled, or after a melting glacier has bared the soil. They are among the last plants to die after man has introduced the poisonous smoke of his factories. When you stare at the face of a lichen, you can often see the shapes of fanciful creatures.

Lichens grow in two dimensions; dandelion seed heads and sea urchins grow in three. These organisms are globular.

Volcanic rock lichens (genus *Physcia*)

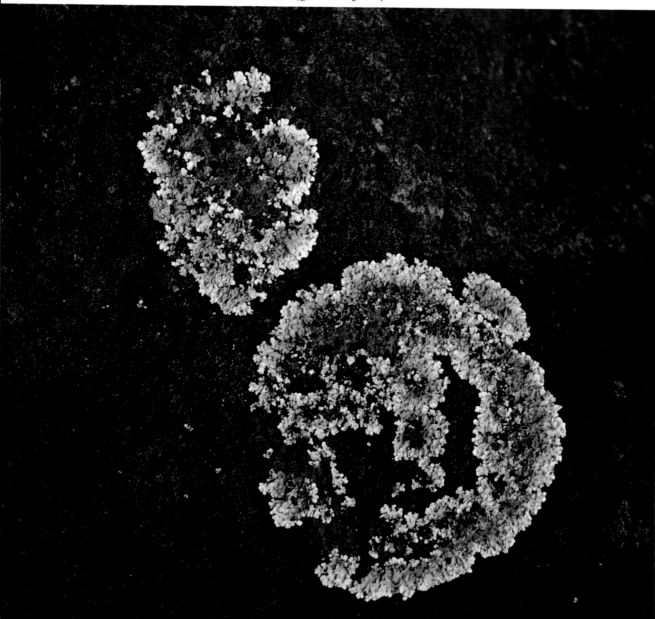

Seed heads of dandelions
(*Taraxacum officinale*)

Red sea urchin
(*Strongylocentrotus
  franciscanus*)

Pearly nautilus (*Nautilus pompilius*)

The sea urchin is related to the starfish. Its ancestors have never lived anywhere but in the sea. It has not changed its spherical shape for more than a hundred million years. Scientists believe that its form has "trapped" it. That is, it never developed a sense of direction—a head, a tail, and right-and-left sides—as did some of its ancient wormlike relatives whose descendants evolved into the higher animals and man.

As the pearly nautilus, a kind of sea snail, grows in size, it builds a series of new rooms each larger than the last. If you were to cut through the shell of a full-grown animal you would find thirty or more rooms. The border of the shell itself describes a logarithmic spiral, a universal growth curve in plant and animal life. It seems to end in a straight line but never quite does. Modern computers can draw pictures of real shells and also pictures of beautiful "shells" that have never existed.

16

You can see the logarithmic spiral at the tip of an unfolding fern leaf—the so-called fiddlehead. If you have a very fast camera and the right kind of light, you can catch the motion of a breaking wave; it too describes a logarithmic spiral.

When simple forms are repeated they bring to the eye the kind of pleasure that music brings to the ear. You can see rhythmic lines when you look at a feather through a hand lens (below, left) or at the shadows cast by a fern (below, right).

Rhythm and repetition are everywhere in nature. Scientists have counted the thin layers in clam shells representing lines of

Feather of a Steller jay
(*Cyanocitta stelleri*)

Shadow of a fern (*Pteridium aquilinum*) on the trunk of a madrona (*Arbutus menziesi*)

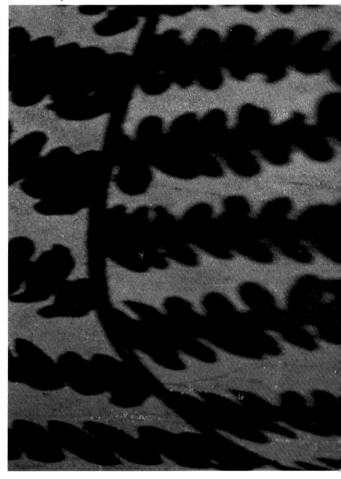

Trillium (*Trillium ovatum*)

daily and yearly growth. They have counted similar layers on fossil clams. The ancient clams had fewer lines in a year's growth than do the modern ones. This strange fact is evidence that when the earth was young it spun on its axis faster than it does today.

The rhythmic form of a plant or animal is called its symmetrical plan. As shown here, the basic plan of the trillium has three axes, or three main sets of angles; that of the dogwood flower has four; that of the apple (seen here in section through the core) has five; that of the wasp nest has six. All natural symmetries are multiples of two, three, or five. Though some starfishes have seven, eleven, or fourteen arms, every starfish begins life as a five-sided embryo.

18

Right, Korean
dogwood (*Cornus* species);
below, left, apple core,
equatorial section, seeds
removed; below, right, the
empty nest of a yellow-jacket
wasp (*Vespa* species)

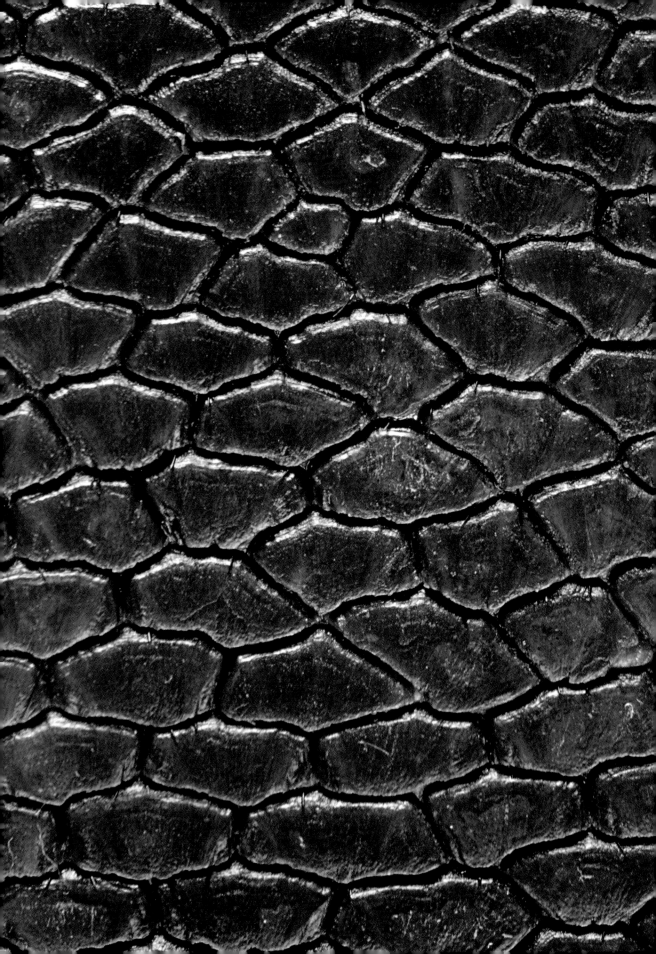

The mosaic pattern at left contains many six-sided (hexagonal) units. Would you have guessed that it represents the tail of a beaver?

The six-sided unit is common in nature wherever close packing on a flat surface is required. The beaver tail needs to be flexible and yet strong; the hexagon is the ideal answer to this architectural problem.

If the hexagon is the ideal unit for filling two-dimensional space, what kind of packages, all alike, would be needed to fill three-dimensional space? In nature, there are many situations where close packing is necessary, as among plant cells in a leaf and air pockets in a lung. Scientists have found one fascinating answer: a unit with fourteen faces, two of which are four-sided, eight five-sided, and four six-sided. The unit has a long name: *beta-tetrakaidecahedron*. It might be called the module of life, and it looks like this:

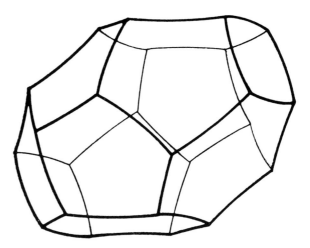

Section of the top of the tail of a beaver (*Castor canadensis*)

Web of grass spider (family *Agelenidae*) from a distance

Texture

Texture is the second element of beauty. You can think of it as form on a smaller scale. It describes the finer parts of a pattern. When you see a spider web at a distance (left) you think of its texture, but when you look closely at one (below) you think of its form.

Spider web, close-up

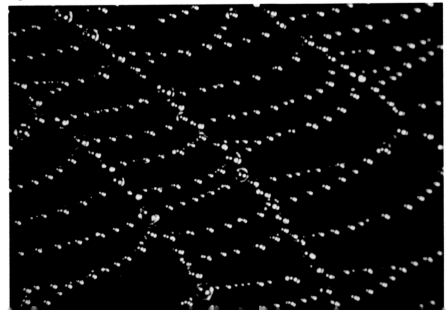

Similarly, as you bring your eye closer to the bark of a tree (right) you gradually lose the feeling of texture and begin to see bold lines and curves. Now you understand how form and texture are related by scale.

Make a circular peephole with your thumb and forefinger; look at different areas of this picture. Turn the book upside down. You will understand why writers have said that beauty is in the eye of the beholder.

Texture is created by surface structure. It invites you to feel with your fingers (if the object is smooth and dry) or warns you not to touch (if the object is prickly or slimy).

Carry a hand lens into a forest and look closely at the miniature gardens of mushrooms, mosses, and lichens on rotten logs. The texture of the dome of a mushroom (below) looks like the street map of a city that has grown too fast.

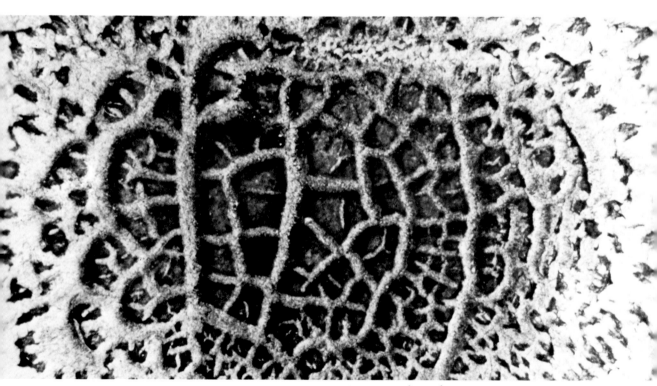

Giant agaric (*Agaricus augustus*), twice enlarged

24

The bark of a madrona tree (*Arbutus menziesi*) in midwinter

Fresh snow on tree branches

Delicate textures are created by the tracery of snow and frost in a forest.

Frost on fallen leaves

Shell fragments on the seacoast

The seashore is rich in textures. Sand, shells, seaweeds, and driftwood are sculptured and moved about and woven together by wind and water.

Before you tramp across a drift of shell fragments (above) to hear them crunch and tinkle, stop for a moment and marvel at the way nature has arrayed them.

Or lie flat on the beach and study the sand beneath your nose. The polished grains shown below were photographed in a small matchbox.

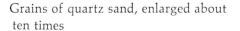

Grains of quartz sand, enlarged about
 ten times

The textures of the ocean are older than life itself. The sight and sound and smell of the sea are deeply rooted in our racial memory.

Surf pattern

Texture on the desert: This looks like a line of cliffs, but the "cliffs" are in reality a sandbank beside a road. It is only as high as a man's head and will survive but a few days in spring, between snowmelt and the coming of the first drying winds.

Sandbank along a roadside

Here are three animal textures: the lumpy skin of a toad (below), the smooth eggs of a robin (right, above), and the jagged teeth of a garden mole (right, below).

A house cat will sometimes kill a mole, then drop it in distaste because of its odor. Insects will quickly find the carcass, nibble away the flesh, and expose the forty sharp teeth. These organs are beautifully adapted for seizing live worms and grubs.

The common toad (*Bufo boreas*)

Nest and eggs of the American robin (*Turdus migratorius*)

Skull of a Townsend mole (*Scapanus townsendi*)

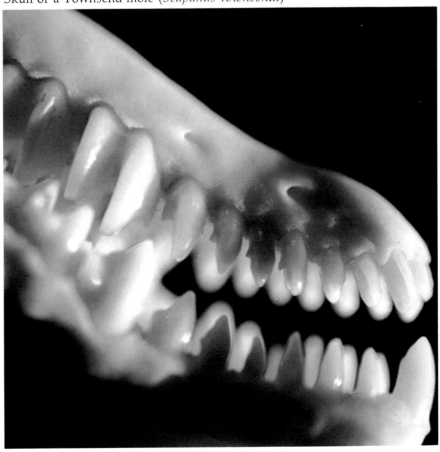

A sea wall at low tide

Color

Color is the third element of beauty. On the left is a scene rich in color: a sea crevice at low tide. The mouths of the green anemones are closed. Pale purple algae cover the rocks like a crust. Red sponges add a touch of brilliance. Below, a starfish waits for the return of the tide, resting like a weary dancer. The

Starfish (*Pisaster ochraceus*)

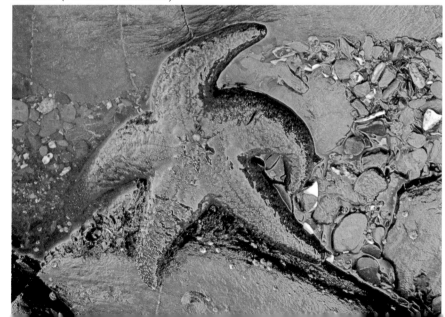

animal itself is blue, and the wet rocks around it seem blue from skylight. The color of any thing is partly its own and partly borrowed from the ever-changing light that strikes it.

Of course you know what color is, but can you define it without using a color word, such as red or blue? In simplified terms, color is the sensation that is created visually in the mind by the wavelengths of light rays.

The artist and the scientist agree that color has three real and measurable qualities. These are:

Hue, which designates a specific color. A hue cannot be described. It must be learned from a teacher. Through experience we learn that the hue of grass is green, that the hue of a fire engine is red, that snow is white and soot is black.

Brightness, which refers to the relative absence of black from a color. A fire engine is bright red and of high brilliance; its color contains little black. A dark-red brick contains black and is of low brilliance.

Saturation, which refers to the relative absence of white from a color. The fire-engine color contains little white; it is highly saturated. Red chalk used in the classroom is pastel red; it contains some white and is low in saturation.

White is a color, too. The phantom orchid (right) is called white because it scatters all the daylight that reaches it. It neither absorbs nor reflects any particular color. Sunlight, though it seems to be white, is a mixture of many colors. We know this because we can see in a rainbow sunlight split into bands of color by droplets of water. The rainbow contains all colors except reddish purple, a color which man can create.

Phantom orchid (*Cephalanthera austinae*)

35

Sunset and wild cherry in winter   Petrified bone of a dinosaur, polished section

Two common kinds of color in nature are shown above. The red of the sunset is a structural color produced by the bending and scattering of light; the red of the rock is a pigment color produced by selective absorption of all hues in light except red.

Structural colors are often temporary, as in a rainbow. Pigment colors are more durable. You can grind up a rock rich in iron oxide (nearly the same thing as rust) and get a reddish pigment that will last for thousands of years.

A third kind of color is generated color, exemplified by the incandescent blue of the lightning flash, the shimmering pastels of the aurora borealis (northern lights), the greenish glow of the firefly, and the faint luminescence (foxfire) of fungi on rotting wood.

The brilliant hues of a butterfly wing and of mother-of-pearl in a mollusk shell are structural colors. If you were to pour

Wing of a tropical butterfly (*Morpho menelaus*)

gasoline on the butterfly wing, the blue would turn brown until the liquid evaporated, when the wing would again look blue. The colors of the shell will gradually fade under bright sunlight as the chemicals change their positions.

Shell of an abalone (*Haliotis fulgens*)

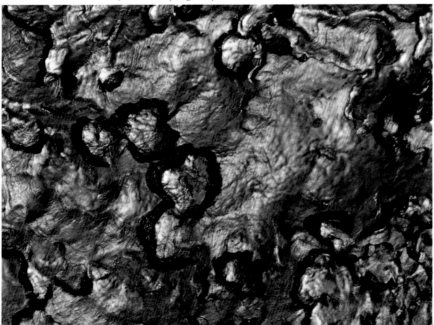

Here is an ancient sedimentary rock stained by its chemicals.

Bedrock on the seacoast

Here are more examples of pigment colors—in a fungus, in a fruit, and in a flower.

Fungus, sulfur polypore (*Polyporus sulfureus*)

Salmonberry (*Rubus spectabilis*)

Alpine forget-me-not (*Eritrichium* species)

Blood starfish (*Henricia leviuscula*)

Leaves change color in autumn because the chemicals within them change. The green-leaf pigment (chlorophyll) breaks down; it has no further work to do. Sugars drain off into the branches, trunk, and roots.

Pigment colors: in a starfish (above) and in the eggs of a crab (below). The rich orange color of the crab eggs is produced by *carotene*, a pigment also present in the flesh and eggs of salmon and in carrots.

Hairy crab (probably *Telmessus*) with eggs

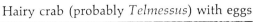

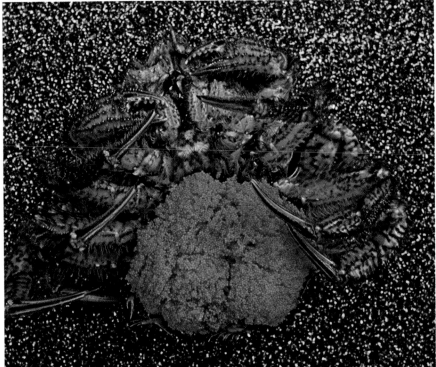

California sea lions (*Zalophus californianus*)

Most mammals, like the California sea lions above and the white-footed mouse below, are dressed in shades of black, white, gray, or brown. One reason is that many mammals have poor color vision. If a mouse can't see color clearly, why should he be colored? Another reason is that plain, somber colors help the mammals to hide from their enemies. Unobtrusive or blending coloration is called camouflage. The primate mammals, including man, have good color vision, and some of them are brilliantly colored. The mandrill monkey has bare skin patches of blue and flaming red, set off by orange fur. Humans can identify, and have given names to, hundreds of colors.

White-footed mouse
(*Peromyscus maniculatus*)

42

Boulders at low tide

Form . . . texture . . . color . . .

Lichens with fruiting spores (*Cladonia coccifera* and *Stereocaulon* species)

Go out now and look for beauty and look for meaning within beauty.

44

Forest reflections in a stream

Go out and use the seeing eye.

45

How the Camera Can Help Your Seeing Eye

Photography can preserve the beauty of outdoor patterns and so prolong your enjoyment of them. Camera stores have many booklets on technique; here are a few ideas that may be useful in approaching the special subject of nature-pattern photography.

Rise early. Go out in the morning when the air is clean and the wind has not begun to blur the leaves, and the light is throwing long shadows that help you create the illusion of depth. Water pools are unruffled; they offer the chance to mirror your subject. Sand patterns on the ocean beach have not been disturbed by footprints or motorcycle treads.

Squint. Judge the value of the composition by shutting one eye and squinting the other. Your lashes will filter out the weak elements, permitting the strong forms and colors to come through. You will see with monocular (one-eye) vision, as the camera does.

Use daylight. Value the richness of natural lighting, even though you may own a fancy flash-lamp outfit guaranteed to illuminate your subject "perfectly." Shadows, as well as lit surfaces, have value in composition. A pattern only suggested holds more interest than one fully explained by a flash.

You may, however, want to change the natural lighting. If a white mushroom is growing under a forest canopy, it will look green. You may be content to photograph it green, but if you insist that it be white, you can use a reddish filter in front of your lens, or use a flash lamp, or move the mushroom into the sunlight. Consult a book on filters if you are interested in capturing true colors. One very useful filter is a polarizing screen. It

46

can add strength to the blue of the sky and cut the surface reflection from wet rocks or shiny leaves. However, you can't always predict whether a composition will be more interesting after it is pola-screened; the shine may be part of its beauty.

Be steady. Use a tripod whenever possible. If the wind is strong, place a rock on your camera. If you are making an exposure longer than one second, be sure that your tripod is not standing in quicksand, or mud, or slowly settling leaf-mold.

Learn your film. Keep to one or two brands and learn how to use them, instead of switching every time you read an advertisement for a new film. Someday, without warning, you may see a handsome pattern and it will be an advantage to be able to set your camera adjustments quickly without thinking. You will learn, too, the limitations of the dyes in your film. These reproduce imperfectly the real colors of nature. For example, the dark purple of the lupine flower does not come out well on a certain popular brand of film.

Use film freely. Often you will have to work fast, and only later will you know what you have captured. The sunlight may be changing, or the tide may be creating a variety of patterns, or a flock of birds may be drifting through the scene. Snap! Snap! Snap! The cost of the film is a small part of your expense in the field. When later you tackle the job of sorting your pictures, be firm. Shed no tears as you throw away half of them. Try for quality, not quantity.

Be alert for the breaks. "Chance favors the prepared mind," Louis Pasteur said. As you walk along a trail you may see a tree that has fallen and lodged at an angle against others. Perhaps you can climb it and aim your camera straight down at some pattern rarely photographed from above. Or you may see an unusual jumble of rocks, among which you will find a flower that you have not seen along the trail. In a windblown tangle of logs you may find a cluster of mushrooms just right for the eye of the camera. You may hear the trickle of water; perhaps it will lead you to a fairyland of ferns and mosses. Once I was drawn by a *smell*. The source was a magnificent cluster of polypores (page 39).

Understand the long lens. A long (or telephoto) lens can be useful even when you are able to get close to your subject. It can help you to capture the mass effect of a field of dandelions (page 15). It can pile up the background, making a distant mountain as important to the camera as to your eye. It can blur the background when you want to emphasize an object in the foreground.

Look for complexity. Though a photograph of a single flower or a polished pebble may be attractive, the most exciting compositions are those that stimulate your imagination and draw you again and again to study their makeup. I do not mean that a pattern should invite you because it is "busy," but rather because it has a certain complexity, a layer-upon-layer effect that asks you to look deeper and deeper into its content.

And, finally, experiment. When you have advanced to developing your own pictures, you can have fun with negatives and color slides. The picture below is a print made by projecting a color slide directly onto enlarging paper, as though it were a negative. This same slide is reproduced in color on page 26.